AF524466

Acknowledgement

First and foremost, I would like to acknowledge the creative energy that permeates this cosmos. Life, the universe, and everything in between has been, and will always be, my biggest muse but it is this creative energy that allows me to express the love and awe that I feel for it.

The creative energy writes through me to expresses its admiration for life; I am merely the conduit of this expression. It is this energy which has given birth to this book. It is this energy which has expressed the intangible and ephemeral. It is this energy which has crafted the rhythm and written the rhymes. All the poems have come through me and not from me, for which I am ever so grateful.

As I continue to dole out gratitude, I would like to appreciate the usual suspects; my family, friends, (ex) partner, and all others who have inspired the poems directly or indirectly.

In particular, I would like to thank my parents, Mamta and Mahesh as well as my sister, Raveena, who have been a source of undying motivation and support.

Divya, my (ex) partner who, so effortlessly, planted the seeds of many poems in the soil of my subconscious and taught me to nurture them. Who taught me not only of life between pages but outside them as well.

Khushboo, who I have never met but who has believed in my poems more than I ever have. Who imbued me with the courage and desire to push these poems out into the world.

All my other friends who, grudgingly, provided invaluable and critical feedback on the poems. Finally, I would also like to express my appreciation for each and every individual with whom I have crossed paths in the walk of life, for they have left their indelible imprint on me, and therefore on the book.

WHY I WRITE POETRY

All through high school and college, I actively avoided language classes. I found it incredulous that people could derive joy from literature; that people would find it fascinating to read and draw squiggly lines. The universe, it seems, has a penchant for irony.

The first time I wrote without any compulsion or obligation, I fell in love with writing. The first time I read a book of my own accord, I could not pull myself away.

MEDITATIVE BEGINNINGS

I took up writing just as I was giving up on meditation. Meditation had been my attempt to quieten the noise inside my head so that I could hear the answers that I was convinced were drowned out by the cacophony.

The noises screamed louder and answers only led to more questions. Writing allowed me to perform a "brain dump", to quell the noise reverberating through my head; it gave me the freedom to splatter my mind onto the page. Writing consumed me and my mornings and I happily gave in.

Prose could easily express the tangible but it struggled with the intangible and that is where poetry came to the rescue. *Poetry is nothing but words that band together in peculiar patterns to point to something beyond themselves. It breathes life into words. It allows them to paint surrealistic paintings without colors and create symphonies without sound. Through poetry, words say nothing and yet, they utter everything.* Poetry has been, not only a savior but a teacher. It has taught me a few things about life.

SURRENDER

I have never managed to write poetry whenever I have actively tried. I can force out prose but never poetry; it moves to its own rhythms and rhymes (pun intended)

My better poems have been the ones that I have not tried to write. They have flown out of me naturally, like a river from a glacier. They have come through me and not from me. Only those poems have been an authentic expression of myself and, therefore, an authentic expression of the universe itself. What are we if not the universe expressing itself in myriad ways.

Like poetry, life can also only be "written" through the powerful act of surrender. Trust the universe to take the right action and allow it to work through you. The right action happens at the right time when you give yourself up.

When you do not allow your ego to dig its claws into the activity. Then, the action comes through you and not from you. It is, what Zen calls, *wu wei or actionless action. The lines between your conscious and subconscious aren't blurred, they are nonexistent. In this state, you are not so far up your head that you become your undoing. In this state, there is total abandonment. In this state, you are not. In this state, you do not become, you be.*

<u>"For all life is an act of faith and an act of gamble"</u>

— — Alan Watts

ALOGICAL

Poetry is neither logical nor illogical; it is alogical. The same could be said of life. Prose, on the other hand, is draped in logic. It has structure and rules that can be bent but not broken. Poetry and life should not be and cannot be defined, cannot be boxed in.

Poetry and life are free-flowing, constantly shattering the shackles that try to tie them down. They are like pieces of a puzzle that never interlock and yet somehow fit. They form a picture that is not perfect but gorgeous nonetheless. Poetry and life can only be accessed by reaching that place that lies beyond cold logic and raw emotion. Both of them are emergent and synergistic properties of logic and emotion; born of the two but belong to neither.

"A mind all logic is like a knife all blade. It makes the hand bleed that uses it."

– Rabindranath Tagore

A POEM IS NOT THE POINT OF POETRY

A poem, like life, cannot be rushed. The point of poetry is not the poem. The point of poetry is just to write. It is the process and not the product that imparts meaning and infuses joy. If you write to "finish" a poem then you are missing out on the point of poetry.

No piece of art is ever complete; that is the best and worst thing about art. Every piece starts is born from the insatiable yearning to create which consumes every artist.

Every piece ends with a partial, and temporary, satiation of that urge as the artist carves out a piece of themselves and calls it art. There is joy in completing a poem but it is the journey of poetry that is frustrating and satisfying all at once.

Life, like poetry, cannot be rushed. The point of life is not to arrive at some destination, it is to be here and reside in the now. The idea is to be in a state of constant departure while always arriving.

Our lives have become a fallacious struggle to reach elusive end results ever faster. We desire fabricated destinations while skipping the journey through whatever means is possible. Poetry has taught me to enjoy this moment without thinking about where it leads. There is nothing to win or lose in life. I am here, I am alive. That is my victory, that is my prize.

"When we make music we don't do it to reach a certain point, such as the end of the composition. If that were the purpose of music then obviously the fastest players would be the best. Also, when we are dancing we are not aiming to arrive at a particular place on the floor as on a journey. When we dance, the journey itself is the point, as when we play music the playing itself is the point."
— — Alan Watts

THE BLANK PAGE AND FEAR OF ACTION

A blank page; that dreaded white vortex is a writer's most formidable foe. It is daunting and intimidating because the writer does not know how to fill it in and where to begin. It can, however, also be a writer's most trusted ally because he does not how to fill it in and where to begin. It can be liberating and inspiring all at once. The page allows him unabated freedom to write anything, anyhow. Limitless, scary potential to create anything he desires.

Life is a blank page and given the deluge of choices in this age, we all face decision paralysis. There are all sorts of pens, input devices, and even different types, colors, and sizes of pages. Don't focus too much on the choices. None of them are wrong and all of them are right.
Understand that you are only distracting yourself with choices not because you are confused but because you are afraid. Call procrastination by its right name, call it fear and begin.

You are not as confused about how to begin as you are fearful about how you will end. You are more concerned not about how to start but about how you will end. You are not concerned about the process but the product. Drop all of that and simply begin.

There is no right or wrong way to write. There is no correct way to begin. The page is only empty until you start writing. Life is only scary until you start living. Get out of your head and arrive on the page of life.

"Nobody ever figures out what life is all about, and it doesn't matter. Explore the world. Nearly everything is really interesting if you go into it deeply enough."
— — Richard P. Feynman

One day your pen will run out of ink and the journal will run out of pages. One day you will run out of time. Do not delay action because you are afraid of failure. Take action because you are afraid of having never tried. Of being filled with regrets. Of never having arrived on the page. Of never having written that poem. Of not living that life. Everyone is capable of splashing words on a piece of paper but only a poet is willing to distill it into a poem. Everyone is capable of being alive but very few are capable of living.

MIND

Mind

Never is my mind
Where it's supposed to be
Always on the move
Running away from me

Between the future and past
Into that void, it strays
Hides in cold comfort
While the present decays

Unfaithful to thoughts
Never stays with one
Romancing many
Is its idea of fun

Master of procrastination
Yet it never slogs
From task to task it jumps
Like a hyperactive frog

Rise above the mind
Above all it craves
It makes for a terrible master
But an excellent slave

Power of the mind

If only you knew
Of the power within
You'd come to realize
That negativity is a sin

The intelligence of the cosmos
Is within every cell
The powers of the universe
Within you dwell

Drop that internal chatter
Then you shall find
The fathomless potential
The power of your mind

Then you will be wary
Of every word that you utter
Then you will watch
Every idea that you mutter

The life that you create
The reality that you reap
It is nothing but
The thoughts that you speak

The world within
Is the world without
You are your creator
Was there ever any doubt?

The force that moves you
Moves the oceans and the sun
Its forms are myriad
But its essence is one

It creates you
And you, it tears down
Lets you soar starry skies
Or buries you underground

Brim with positivity
Glitter like morning light
If you succumb to the darkness
How will you escape the night?

You are the observer
Relinquish all control
You are the creator, the destroyer
Be the half to be the whole

Thoughts

Why do you dart around
Hunting your thoughts all day
And when you do catch them
Why do you let them slip away

Through all this mad sprinting
What do you hope to find
Thoughts leave behind no answers
Only a breathless mind

To regain control
Resist all urge
Sit back and observe
Unless your thoughts you wish to serve

You are chasing shadows
When each thought you follow
Can't you see it yet
All thoughts are hollow

End this neurosis
Stop, drop, take a pause
You are a symptom of your thoughts
You are not their cause

LESSONS

Magic

Look around
It is all fleeting
All in passing
Won't keep repeating

It comes together
Only to dissipate
Doesn't stay long
With death, it has a date

It all begins
Only to end
There comes the free fall
After the ascend

No moment ever lasts
It slides like sand
Savor it while you can
As it slips from your hand

It cannot be grasped
To it, you must surrender
Become one with the moment
To realize its splendor

Some term it sad
Others call it tragic
That nothing lasts forever
So I call it magic

Home

Home is not
Where you stay
Where you return
At the end of the day

Home is not
Where you've lived long
Time counts for nothing
Home is where you belong

Home is not a place
But a feeling earned
It is never a home
If to it you must return

Who believes she has left home
Has already come back
Never will she be complete
Sensing a nagging "lack"

Home is an idea
A thought in your mind
Home is not something
You leave behind

Live in the now
Make every moment your home
Surrender to it
So unfettered you may roam

Ikigai

Life is nothing
But a search for Ikigai
Your reason for being
Your answer to why

If you have a "why"
You can bear any "how"
If you have a why
You are one with the

What is it that moves you
What do you desire
What is that completes you
What burns that inner fire

Question, seek, wonder
Never be content
Follow your curiosity
Ikigai awaits at the end

Discover your own tune
Dance to your own song
If you look at others
You won't know where you belong

You are questioned by life
YOUR meaning you are asked
And when you believe the answer
You've found Ikigai at last

Let

Let your breath move you
Let it fill every space
Let it roam freely
Let it set the pace

Let your pulse move you
Let it define the beat
Let it set the tempo
Let you and it accrete

Let your thoughts move you
Let them ideate
Let them birth ideas
Let them create

Let your spirit move you
Let it take control
Let it decide action
Let it make you whole

Find myself there

If I continue holding on
I will never be free
If I refuse to let go
I will never be me

I am neither my emotions
Nor am I my beliefs
Neither my fleeting happiness
Nor my sticky grief

I am not my exhilarating ecstasy
Nor my crippling pain
I am beyond it all
I am, when nothing remains

If the future I carry
And the past I don't leave behind
Then no matter where I go
Myself I won't find

These torturing thoughts
And feelings that spook and scare
They will haunt me
Till I don't become aware

For if I was
Then I would see
Life demands nothing
Except to just be

To simply let go
To be naked and bare
To move beyond questions
And find myself there

Listen to music

Listen to music
You won't need any answers
Listen to music
Life is an act and we are dancers

Listen to music
And you will be found
Listen to music
And heal yourself with sound

Listen to music
And be in a trance
Listen to music
And continue to dance

Listen to music
To find your voice
Listen to music
And without reason rejoice

Listen only to the music
Drown in it, submerge
Listen only to the music
It is the language of the universe

There are no mistakes

There are no mistakes
There are lessons to learn
A puzzle with a prize
Which you'll have to earn

There are no mistakes
Why do you hold on tight
Living in the past
Is not going to make them right

There are no mistakes
Unless you repeat
Then it is a mistake
And it has you beat

This when you are that

You cannot hustle
Till you learn to relax
You cannot accelerate
Till you learn to slack

You cannot love
Till you accept you can hate
Can't show up on time
Till you are perpetually late

You cannot be serious
Till you learn how to play
You cannot listen
Till you drop the need to say

The pleasure of eating
Is learned when you fast
For you to be first
Someone had to be last

You cannot arrive
Till you learn how to depart
You cannot use your head
Till you feel with your heart

You cannot win
Without learning to lose
Can't understand the other

Till you walk in their shoes

You learn to be selfish
Before you turn kind
Only when you lose
Do you know what to find

You learn to move
By staying perfectly still
Being shattered and tattered
Teaches you how to will

You learn to live
By experiencing death
Learn how to breathe
When you run out of breath

You learn to be present
By being where you are at
Learn to be all of this
By understanding, you are that

They are it

It took a while
Longer than I would admit
To come to realize
That they are it

Life was a puzzle
And as I looked for pieces that fit
I came to understand
That they are it

To nothing else, you need submit
To nothing else, you need commit
To them, give everything
For they are it

They will pull you out
Of this chasmic existential pit
Onto the plains of meaning
For they are it

A flash of their smile
And every moment is lit
All darkness consumed
For they are it

Don't search for the answers
With your sense and wit
Feel it with your heart
To know that they are it

Simmer your bonds
Bit by tiny bit
Eventually it will dawn
That people ***ARE IT***

QUESTIONS

&

ANSWERS

Question

There is this question
Eternal and old
It does not have an answer
Only lies to be told

Why does life exist
What is its role
What is the purpose
What is the end goal

Ponder it deeply
Drop all convictions
Exploit your logic
Restrict all emotions

The answer will become obvious
As you drown in fear
There is all for nothing
That'll be painfully clear

Your facade of meaning
Will swiftly crumble
Your world will be chaos
Utterly jumbled

Stick with the question
Let yourself be possessed
Move beyond thinking
There is more to this quest

Guided by intuition
Turn the question inside out
Abandon reasoning
Expunge all doubt

The answer will become obvious
As you drown in bliss
This is all for everything
You judged amiss

What do you choose?

What do you choose?
To react or respond?
To be chained by habits
Or to break those bonds?

What do you choose?
Compulsion or choice?
To echo the others
Or to listen to your voice?
What do you choose?
Hedonism or health?
Distractions of the world
Or your inner wealth?

What do you choose?
Patience or pleasure?
Instant gratifications
or hidden treasures?
What do you choose?
Matter or mind?
To carry the past
or leave it all behind?

What do you choose?
Silence or sound
To surf above the noise
or to comfortably drown?

What do you choose?

Discipline or desire?
To stay on the ground
Or soar ever higher?
What do you choose?
To survive or strive?
Do you choose to live
Or do you choose to be alive?

When?

When can a boy
Be called a man?
How does a thought
Grow into a plan?

When can a seed
Be called a tree?
How many drops
Make a mighty sea?

When do men
Discover their desire?
How does it spark
That eternal fire?

When does a student
Begin to teach?
How much sand
Before it's a beach?

When does silence
Begin to speak?
How does a day
Turn into a week?

When can a cell
Be called alive?
How many of them
Before you term it life?

When do I stop looking
So that I can see?
How do I unbecome
All that has become me?

When do I surrender
To set me free?
How do I disappear
So that I can be?

INSPIRATION

Fight

Never ever tire
Never ever stop
If you can't run
You continue to walk

You arrive at the page
You show up to the fight
Your life's story
No one else can write

In the dark of the night
With no victory in sight
When nothing seems right
And you're numbed with fright

Gather you might
Put up a fight
Grow wings, take flight
Be your own light

With wars and battles
Every day is rife
The choice is yours
A hero's death
Or a coward's life

I will

I will compete
I will fight
I will never give up
Till I make it right

I will not halt
Even when I stumble
I will not cease
Even when I fumble

I will resist
I will rage
I will break free
From this mental cage

I will not tire
Won't accept defeat
Even if I have to
Bring destiny to its feet

I will not crumble
I will not crack
Perseverance will cover
For all that I lack

I will persist
I will not quit
I will break through
Bit by tiny bit

I will not back down
Society is strife
I will wage war
I will choose life

Word constipation

All those who write
Are vulnerable to a condition
Some call it writer's block
I prefer "word constipation"

Strikes without warning
For no specific duration
Words just won't come out
There is absolute cessation

The word-smith strains
And the word-smith struggles
But all in vain
For there are no words to juggle

But the moment he stops
He gains insight
Stepping out of his head
He rediscovers how to write

You write without writing
You let the words speak
Words always find the writers
There's no need to seek

Allow the words to flow
Even if you are full of doubts
Even if the words feel like shit
At least they are coming out

SPIRIT

I am (I)

I am every age
I have ever been
I am every person
I have ever seen

I am every experience
I have ever had
The fierce, the feeble
The good, especially the bad

I am every song
I have ever heard
I am every book
The logical and the absurd

I am every thought
I have ever thought
I am every yearning
I have ever sought

I am every nightmare
And all my dreams
I am my laughter
And all my screams

I am every deed
Every horrid and wonderful act
When I respond
More so when I react

I am every idea
The tangible and the abstract
Every broken promise
Every honored pact

I am my hopes
And all my fears
I am my enemies
And my peers

I am my losses
And all my wins
I am my virtues
And even my sins

I am all
And so I am none
I am multitudes
And so I am one

I am (II)

I am a universe formed
A new star being born

I am that star collapsing and dying
And its stardust which through space is flying

I am the planets around the star revolving
And the life on them forever evolving

I am the comets through the cosmos zipping
And the probes which are through them ripping

I am a galaxy formed as the stars unite
And the blasts of radiation when galaxies get too tight

I am the dark energy that everywhere resides
And the dark matter which in plain sight hides

I am the lava, the seas, the mountain
The thunder, snow, and the rain

I am that which animates the inanimate
I am that which decides all fates

Life is...

Life is a page
Blank and white
Waiting to be filled
With stories that you write

Life is a path
You must fearlessly stray
Without being lost
Who has ever found their way?

Life is a journey
Without a destination
There's nowhere to be
It's a nomadic vacation

Life is theatre
We've all got our parts
It is an act
To be played with soul and heart

Life is a game
Of illusions and lies
Nothing to lose or gain
Life is the prize

Many names

Dark gives birth to light
Day brings forth the night

Silence gives way to sound
Only the lost are ever found

Cold is an expression of hot
Every line begins as a dot

All geniuses are insane
Only in loss there is gain

Front brings forth the back
White is the same as black

Peace is sought through strife
Death births new life

Every right is a wrong
The weak give rise to the strong

Yang has always mirrored yin
We lose so that we may win

Every opposite is the same
We have just given them
Many names

THE ANIMATE AND THE INANIMATE

Flame

Become like the flame
Calm unwavering bonding

Become like the flame
Never reacting only responding

Become like the flame
Giving but never expecting

Become like the flame
Dispelling darkness with light

Become like the flame
Never giving up without a fight

Become like the flame
Burning till the end with all its might

Become like the flame
Illuminating the wrong and the right

Become like the flame
Taking every moment as something new

Become like the flame
And let the flame become you

Lizard

There sits on my wall
A great green lizard
Appears innocuous
But he is a zen wizard

Motionless and still
Yet fully aware
Senses razor sharp
With a penetrating stare

Bides his time
Till the moment is right
Darts off quickly
Taking majestic flight

He does not choose
Lets the action appear
Never any doubt
His mind is always clear

In this state of zen
Sits that great green lizard
Glazed in magic
He is the wild wizard

About the Author

Ravishu is curiosity personified; there is no better way to capture his essence. A self-described neophile, his search for novelty extends from his innate desire to know and understand life, universe and everything in between.

This desire has propelled him to constantly question everything within existence. While most questions have carried their own answer within them, there are certain questions that are bereft of answers, including life itself.

Ravishu might have an arsenal of literary devices at his disposal but poetry has always been his weapon of choice to slice open questions that refuse to reveal an answer; to write about the that which cannot be penned down and to talk about that which cannot be said.

"(Be)lieve" features poems from a place beyond logic, reason and thought. A place within the psyche of every conscious being. A place that is free of cognition and thought. A place of unadulterated belief; of pure faith.

The book started off as an attempt to explain the unanswerable questions of life. As the book evolved, so did the poet. The book, and the poems within it, come from an understanding that the purpose was never to answer the unanswerable questions but to accept their indecipherable nature. The challenge was not to persist but to surrender. The idea was not to unravel the mystery of life but to accept it and be in awe.

This realization comes only through belief. Belief comes only when a person understands how to be. When she gives up the want to become and instead returns to the need to be. When she stops trying to become something and reverts to her original state of being nothing.

Then she can let go off everything else including herself. Then she can be empty and full all at once. Then she can perceive and not merely see. Then she can believe because she can simply be.

Printed by Libri Plureos GmbH in Hamburg, Germany